# ARNIS
# GENERAL
# TERMINOLOGY

**ANGELO TIWANA QUIAMCO**

# ARNIS GENERAL TERMINOLOGY

*Alexiuz Cruz*
Copyright © 2015 by Angelo Tiwana Quiamco

ISBN: 978-1-32-939836-8

Library of Congress Cataloging in Publication Data
Data available

# ARNIS

# GENERAL

# TERMINOLOGY

Compiled by

*Angelo Tiwana Quiameo*

# Preface

Through my experience of writing articles, books, and poems, one thing has been consistent. That thing being that what people want is to be able to improve their lives. Not only do people want to improve their lives, they want to know how, and they want to start soon. May the words and thoughts of these pages be the advice they have been looking for.

The title to this article says it all. Find a hobby and you will discover a life. As being happy is a key ingredient in the factors and necessities of living, having a hobby has its place in our life's story. I can remember when I first found an interest in Arnis back in my high school years. Not only was it fun, it was something that I could do handsome well. It was something that I could do with others and makes training out of a simple time of leisure.

Later in life, as a working adult, Arnis became a hobby for me to relieve stress after work on the weekends. My best friend at the time and I would meet up every Monday to Friday and sometimes on Saturday at our favorite Arnis training field. We would train for two to three hours straight trying to increase our skills, scores, and personal achievements, as well as self-preservation.

The author of this book aim to:

- strengthen and widen the promotions and dissemination of R. A 9850 (ARNIS) the Philippines National Martial Art and Sport;
- upgrade and update knowledge to develop skills in high intellectual and critical operations, more authentic skills and creative strategies;
- develop strong relationship among practitioners of the art with one common goal to serve, protect, promote our own martial arts thus preserving our culture;
- awareness of such values as solidarity, brotherhood, friendship, gratitude, respect, global bond, and national pride; and
- promoting the indigenous martial art of Arnis as a self-defense, sport and cultural discipline.

**Author**

# Acknowledgement

Permission to reprint the following:

**Republic Act 9850**

**Etymology of Arnis**

# CONTENTS

# What is Arnis?

*Arnis General Terminology*

There are many terms that an arnisador, eskrimador, bastoneros and kalisador practitioner needs to know in order to learn ARNIS easily.

These four (4) terms are often used interchangeably to describe the Filipino martial art and sport of the Philippines.

**Arnis** – the most popular Tagalog term used in the Philippines to describe the Filipino martial art and sport. It is derived from the Spanish word "arnes" which means "armor", typically used to describe the stick fighting side of the Arnis.

**BASTON** – refers to Arnis in Panay Island; a hard wooden stick like kamagong, sibukaw and oway or rattan that primarily used effectively for striking and depending oneself from an attacker.

**ESKRIMA**– Spanish word which translates to " fencing.." This term is used in the Visayas region of the Philippines. Like Arnis, it is often used to describe the stick fighting aspect of the art.

**KALI** – term developed by Filipinos in America during the 1950's and 1960's to describe the pre-Hispanic martial art and sport of the Philippine Island. Often used as a term to refer to the bladed arts of the Filipino people.

---

**Arnis** is the **National Martial Art and Sport** of the **Philippines** (**Republic Act 9850**) declared last **December 11, 2009** by **President Gloria Macapagal Arroyo**.

---

## Counting Number

| English | Filipino | Spanish |
|---------|----------|---------|
| one | isa | *uno* |
| two | dalawa | *dos* |
| three | tatlo | *tres* |
| four | apat | *cuatro* |
| five | lima | *cinco* |
| six | anim | *seis* |
| seven | pito | *siete* |
| eight | walo | *ocho* |
| nine | siyam | *nueve* |
| ten | sampo | *diez* |

## Weapons

| English | Tagalog |
|---------|---------|
| Cane | baston |
| Double cane | Doble baston |
| Sword or Cane Butt | Punyo |
| Knife | Punyal |
| Single Cane | Solo Baston |
| Sword | Espada |
| Dagger | Daga |
| Sword and Dagger | Espada y Dagger |
| Bolo | Tabak |
| Yantok | Rattan |
| Iron Reed | Bahi |
| Butterfly Knife | Balisong |
| Staves | Bangkaw |
| Shield | Panangga |
| Indo-Malay Dagger | Kris o Kalis |
| Spear | Sibat |
| Fork-Tipped Sword | Kampilan |
| Chained Sticks | Tabak-Toyok |

# ᛒeneral Terminology

There are many terms that an arnisador, eskrimador, or even bastonero and kalisador need to know in order to learn Eskrima, Kali, Baston and Arnis easily.

| TERMS USED | ENGLISH MEANING |
|---|---|

## A

| | |
|---|---|
| abanico | fan |
| abanico corto | fan strike in short range |
| abanico doblata | double fan strike |
| abanico largo | fan strike in long range |
| abante | move forward |
| abecedario | Spanish for "alphabet" |
| abierta;abierto | open |
| abierto candado | dis-arming technique |
| abilidad | ability |
| alibata | early Filipino writings |
| alisan ng sandata | dis-armed |
| alisto | alert |
| alternativo | alternative |
| agawin | to grab |
| agapayan | parallel |
| aghimo | techniques |
| agimat | amulet |
| agwat | distance |
| albelum | diagonal upward strike |
| aldabis | diagonal downward strike |
| alisaga | random |
| alsahin | to lift up |
| antanda | sign of the cross |
| antangan | design |
| anyo | kata; a presentation and expression of the arts and forms of |

|  | striking, defense, movements, power and speed techniques. |
|---|---|
| Arnisador | male practitioner of the art |
| Arnisadora | female practitioner of the art |
| Arnisadores | pl. form of Arnisadora |
| Arnisadores | pl. form of Arnisador |
| atake | attack |
| atas | command |
| atras | move backward |
| awatin | to restrain |
| away | fight |

## B

| bahaghari | rainbow |
|---|---|
| bahi | heart of the palm |
| balaraw | dagger |
| balakang | hipbone |
| balikat | shoulder |
| baluti | armor |
| banat | strain |
| banda y banda | strike of elasticity |
| baraw | Cebuano term for knife or dagger |
| basisig | centrifugal force |
| baston | cane |
| batiin | to greet; salute |
| batuta | cane use by barangay police |
| baston y daga | cane and dagger |
| bayanihan | cooperation; Filipino term for working together |
| baywang | waist; hip |
| bikaka | a stance where the legs are apart |
| bilis | speed |
| binakoko | long blade named after a porgy fish |
| binti | calf of the leg |
| bitiwan | set loose |
| braso | arm; forearm |
| budlay | difficult |
| bukung-bukong | ankle |

| | |
|---|---|
| buntal | horizontal strike |
| buntala | planet |
| buntala sais | planet six; weaving in center |

## C

| | |
|---|---|
| cinco | five |
| cinco tiero | five combined strike |
| corto | short range |

## D

| | |
|---|---|
| daga | dagger |
| dalusong | high vantage attack |
| dapa | fall lace down |
| daplis | strike in oblique |
| dibdib | chest; thorax |
| dipa | sideward extension |
| doblada | double |
| doblata | double |
| doble baston | double cane |
| doble ekisan | double "x" form strike |
| doble olisi | two sticks |
| doblete | double round strike |
| doce biradas y kombatan porma | twelve combat strike form |
| dulo y dulo | short stick about four to seven inches in length, held in the palm of the hand |
| dumog | Panay term for ground fighting |

## E

| | |
|---|---|
| ehersisyo | exercise |
| ehersisyo na pang palakas ng katawan | power and stamina exercise |
| ekut | handkerchief |
| ekis pababa | "x" downward strike |
| ekis pataas | "x" upward strike |
| ekis y ekis doblata | 2 "x" form strike |

| | |
|---|---|
| entrada | entrance |
| entrampar | catch in a trap |
| esgrema | stick fighting |
| Eskrimador | male practitioner of the art |
| Eskrimadora | female practitioner of the art |
| espada y baston | sword and cane |
| espada y daga | sword and dagger |
| estilo | style |
| estrella | star form strike |

## F

| | |
|---|---|
| florete | twirling strike |

## G

| | |
|---|---|
| galang-galangan | wrist |
| galaw circulo | circular motion |
| galaw ng kamay | hand movements |
| ganting-lusob | counterstrike |
| gapang | crawl; creep |
| garbanzos | dis-armed techniques |
| gawain | activity |
| Ginoo | sir; gentleman |
| gitisig | centripetal force |
| gitnaang distansya | middle range |
| gulugod | backbone; the spine |

## H

| | |
|---|---|
| habi | weave |
| habyog | torgue |
| hache | axe |
| hakbang | step |
| handa | prepare |
| hantad | exposed |
| hatol | justify |
| hating-galaw circulo | semi-circular motion |
| hawak | grip |
| hilaga | north |

| | |
|---|---|
| hilis | diagonal |
| hirada | forward |
| hita | thigh |
| hubad-lubad | from Doce Pares is frequently used as a type of "generator" drill, where one is forced to act and think fast |
| hulwaran | pattern |

## I

| | |
|---|---|
| ibayo | double |
| idalom | nafir |
| igpaw | forward leap |
| ihampas | to strike |
| itak | bolo |
| itsa | to throw |
| Ingratan Gazar | combination of stances and motion Indonesian term used in their martial art internationally called "Pencak Silat". |
| isog | power; with strength |
| ituktok | zenith |
| iunat | to stretch out |

## K

| | |
|---|---|
| kadalumon | depth |
| kailaliman | depth |
| kailalimang anim | weaving form strike; ground six |
| kali daanan | way of the blade |
| kali wala | without blade |
| kaliwa | left |
| kamagong | hard wood; ebony |
| kamot | hand |
| kampilan | fork-tipped sword, popular in the southern Philippines |
| kanan | right |
| kandado | lock |
| kandado sirado | dis-arming lock technique |

| | |
|---|---|
| kanluran | west |
| karga | load |
| kasunduan | agreement |
| katayuan | position |
| korta pluma | pocket knife |
| kris | sword or knife |
| kudkuran | butting strike |
| kuluntoy | curled up |
| kulurete | rouge |
| kurbada | curve downward strike |
| krusada | cross strike form |
| kusog | energy |

# L

| | |
|---|---|
| Labanan | a full contact event in a sportive tournament wherein the two players dressed with body and head protector armed with padded stick |
| Lakambini | a title given to those belonging to the nobility of ancient Filipino; muse |
| Lakan | a title given to those belonging to the nobility of ancient Filipino; escort |
| lakas | strength |
| Laktaw Angulo | footwork; pattern stance |
| langitnin anim | heaven six; weaving form strike |
| laraw | form |
| largo | long range |
| Largo mano yantok | longer stick ranging from twenty-eight to thirty-six inches |
| latigo | spanish for whip |
| lenguwahe | language |
| lihok | motion |
| linangin | develop |
| lingay | to lend the body backward |
| lengua de fuego | butt strike |
| lugay | downward twirling strike |
| luhod | kneel; fall on bended knees |

| | |
|---|---|
| lukso | jump |
| lumpatan | jumping style |

## M

| | |
|---|---|
| Magbigay Pugay! | to give respect; a formal form of respect |
| malapitang distansya | close quarter range |
| malayuang distansya | long quarter range |
| Mano mano | is the empty-hand component of Filipino martial arts, particularly Arnis; hand to hand |
| matapang | brave |
| Mawalang-galang po! | a formal address of "excuse me" |
| memoria | memory |
| midianus | eight middle strike |
| mirasol | flowering strike |

## N

| | |
|---|---|
| ningas | flame |
| ninuno | ancestor |
| nipis | slight contact |
| noo | forehead |
| ngawit | tireness |
| nguso | snout |

## O

| | |
|---|---|
| obra maestra | master piece |
| Opo! | yes sir or mam, a formal answer in affirmative |
| oracion | prayer; angelus |

## P

| | |
|---|---|
| pabilog | circular |
| padron | pattern; model |
| pagdalo | attendance |
| pagsasanay | training or exercise |

| | |
|---|---|
| paha | band; sash |
| pahalang | horizontal |
| pahintulot | permission |
| palad | palm of the hand |
| panangga | shield |
| panga | jaw |
| panganib | danger |
| parasol | umbrella forming strike |
| piktos | a slight strike |
| pilantik | upper heading strike |
| pitik | a three combination of slight strike |
| pagkalutukan | flexibility |
| panuntukan | an empty hand fighting known in Panay |
| pinid | closed |
| pugto | break |

## R

| | |
|---|---|
| rebeño circulo | spiral weaving strike |
| reklamo | complaint |
| redondo | a vertical strike |
| regulasyon | regulation; rules |
| ribonado | ribbon forming strike |
| rompida | up and down |

## S

| | |
|---|---|
| salapang | spear strike |
| sandata | armed weapon or weapon |
| sanduguan | blood compact |
| sanga | block |
| San Miguel | a forehand strike with the right hand, moving from the striker's right shoulder toward their left hip |
| sarong | a length of fabric wrapped around the waist |
| sikad | thrust |
| sinawali | weaving |
| sinawali cinco puntas | weaving flow of 10 strikes |

| | |
|---|---|
| sinawali cuatro puntas | weaving flow of 8 strikes |
| sinawali seis puntas | weaving flow of 12 strikes |
| sibat | javelin |
| siko | elbow |
| silangan | east |
| sinsilyo | a single strike |
| sintas | rope |
| sipa | kick |
| solo baston | single cane |
| sombaganay | an empty hand fighting |
| sperado | double stick drill |
| sperillo | three combinational strike |
| sumaklang | to straddle |
| susi | key |
| suntok | fist |
| sungkiti | thrust |
| sol seis | heaven six; sun six |

## T

| | |
|---|---|
| tabak toyok | chained sticks/ flail; nunchaku |
| tablayan | charge |
| tabon | head blocking form |
| Tagalog | basis of national language of Filipinoes |
| taguan ng sandata | arsenal |
| takay | term |
| tanikala | chain |
| tapihan | deflexive strike |
| tapi-tapi | flow hand drill |
| tibay | endurance |
| tiera seis | Earth six weaving strike |
| tagumpay | victory; triumph |
| tikas | stance |
| tikas ekis | "x" stance |
| tikas pasaklang | straddle stance |
| tikas pusa | cat stance |
| tikas pasulong | forward stance |
| tikas pasulong na pahalang | diagonal forward stance |
| tikas pasulong sa | |

| | |
|---|---|
| gilid | lateral forward stance |
| tikas paurong | back stance |
| tikas paurong na pahalang | diagonal backward stance |
| tikas paurong sa gilid | lateral forward stance |
| timog | south |
| tinaasang anim | sky six; weaving form strike |
| tiwalag | to separate |
| tres primos | three prime striking |
| tuhod | knee |
| tunay | authentic; genuine |
| tuon | focus |
| turnilyantis | screw strike |
| tuwangang pagganap | coordination |

## U

| | |
|---|---|
| uhaw | thirst |
| umiwas | to evade |
| umpog | bump |
| umurong | to go back |
| una | first |
| unahan | front |
| urong | to step back |

## V

| | |
|---|---|
| villa mano | stance with strike |

## W

| | |
|---|---|
| waslik | sweep block |

# Palabras Usada En La Educacion
## Words Used at Training

### *Mga Katawagan sa Pagsasanay*

Parts of the Human Body – Averdo – Katawan

| ENGLISH | FILIPINO | SPANISH |
|---------|----------|---------|
| arm | braso | brazo |
| back | likod | espalda |
| belly | tiyan | vientre |
| brain | utak | seso |
| breast | dibdib | pecho |
| cheek | pisngi | mejilla |
| chin | baba | barba |
| ear | tenga | oreja |
| elbow | elbo | codo |
| eye | mata | oyo |
| eyebrow | kilay | ceja |
| face | mukha | cara |
| finger | daliri | dedo |
| finger nail | kuko | uña |
| forehead | noo | frente |
| hair | buhok | pelo |
| hair | buhok | cabello |
| head | ulo | cabeza |
| ENGLISH | FILIPINO | SPANISH |
| hand | kamay | mano |
| heel | sakong | talon |
| intestine | bituka | tripa |
| knee | tuhod | rodilla |
| leg | hita | perna |
| lung | baga | pulmon |
| mouth | bibig | boca |
| nape | leeg | nuca |
| nipple | utong | teta |
| nose | ilong | nariz |
| palm of the hand | palad | palma |
| shoulder | balikat | hombro |

# Arnis General Terminology

| sole of the foot | sakong | planta |
|---|---|---|
| thigh | hita | muslo |
| tooth | ngipin | diente |
| tongue | dila | lengua |
| ankle | bukong-bukong | tobillo |
| eyelash | pilikmata | pestaña |
| lip | labi | labio |
| heart | puso | corazon |

## Stick Fighting From Different Positions

There are nine (9) general stick combat positions that you and your opponent can engage. They include the following:

- Both you and your opponent are in the facedown position.
- You are kneeling and your opponent is facedown position.
- Your opponent is kneeling and you are facedown position.
- Both you and your opponent are kneeling.
- You are standing and your opponent is facedown.
- Your opponent is standing and your opponent is kneeling.
- Your opponent is standing and you are kneeling.
- Both you and your opponent are standing.

## The Stick Fighting Ranges

There are three (3) separate distances or stick combat that must be completely mastered. They include:

- Close Quarter Stick Combat – this is the distance of stick fighting where you can strike your opponent's with the butt of your weapon and you can employ a variety of knee, elbow and head butt strikes.
- Mid-Range Stick Combat – the intermediate stick fighting range where you can strike your opponent's arm, heads and body with your baston.
- Long Range Stick Combat – the furthest distance you can only strike your opponent's hand with your baston.

# The Three (3) Main Aspects of Arnis

**SPORTIVE** – Arnis as played in tournament is called *"Labanan"*, a full contact event wherein the two players dressed with body and head protector armed with padded stick engage each other in sportive fighting under the rules and regulations set by the tournament organizer.

**CULTURAL** – Arnis is played in unique way through the competition or presentation and expression of the art and forms of striking, movements, power, speed and defense techniques. It is popularly called *"Anyo"*. The player wears appropriate ethnic or sportive attire. The player uses a solo baston, doble baston, *espada y daga* or sword and dagger. It could also be presented in a combination of solo baston and daga or sword and baston. The anyo could be done by solo performer or in group of two or three members in a synchronize manner.

**COMBATIVE** – is the ultimate application of Arnis fighting skills where trainee(s) is are trained for self-defense and self-preservation. This is practical especially for law enforcement agencies to sharpen their skills in keeping peace and order condition.

## Don't Thrust Your Baston Sticks

Avoid performing thrusting motions when stick fighting, thrusting your baston stick can be risky for the following reasons:

- Stick thrusting motions simply lack neutralizing power.

- You can lose your baston stick when impacting with a strong surface are.

- When the tip of your baston contact with a hard body target, it will put enormous strain on your wrists which can lead to a severe sprain or possible break.

- Thrusting motions simply with a baston stick should be used sparingly and only under certain combative circumstances. Generally, thrusting motions should be used when knife fighting.

## Stages of Training and Development

There are three (3) stages of development in Arnis – *operability*, *functionability* and *non-counterability*.

These stages are trained in progression and may overlap, especially during practice of drills that lead into applications.

**Operability** – the stage where you begin to learn to apply and combine all the individual techniques into coordination series of strategy and the movements and tactics behind the techniques are learned and understood.

**Functionability** – the second stage, where everything from footwork to striking mechanics are broken down individually and trained until each one is mastered.

**Non-Counterability** – the third and last stage where you can execute offensive strikes with dynamic footwork in such ways that your opponents are unable to attack in similar attack or defend against your attack.

## S.T.P.A.P
(SPEED, TIMING, POWER, ACCURACY, PRECISION)

There are five (5) physical attributes that a arnisador or bastonero must possess to be effective in combat.

- Speed – an Arnis warrior must be fast in thought, movement and delivery of his striking and attack the opponent first and preventing him from counterattacking.
- Timing – an Arnis warrior must be a master of timing. He must know when to strike and be put out of ranges and counters the enemy if he moves to the same strike. His movements must be unpredictable to the opponent's sight.
- Power – with speed and timing, an Arnis warrior must be able to deliver his attacks with the correct amount of power. He must understand the different energies involved in any strikes in order to be effective.
- Accuracy – along with speed, timing and power, an Arnis warrior must be able to deliver his attacks to specific targets and do so as intended.
- Precision – this is the ability to manipulate your weapon with absolute control during combat.

## Four (4) Defensive Options

During a stick fighting, you only have four (4) possible defensive or offensive options. Make certain you can execute all four of thes response with ease and efficiency when fighting with sibukaw, rattan, kamagong sticks, etc.

- STRIKING – you can strike the opponent's weapon hand with your own stick.
- BLOCKING – you can block the oncoming stick attack.
- DEFLECTION – you can deflect the strike attack.
- EVASION - you can moved out of the angle of the baston attack.

# Keep Your Baston Moving

When  fighting with sticks, always keep your stick or baston moving. This is important for the following reasons:

- It enhances your defensive reaction time.
- It makes your opponent misjudge the range of your baston.
- It minimizes weapon telegraphing, especially prior to striking with your stick.
- It prevents inertia from setting in during combat.
- It enhances the overall velocity of your strikes.
- It enhances your offensive flow.

# Use Different Types of Fighting Sticks

If you want to improve your overall baston combat skills, its important to have your training partner practice with a wide range of sticks. The following are some work-out sticks you can use:

- short sticks
- long sticks
- light sticks
- heavy sticks
- balanced sticks

- unbalanced sticks
- cumbersome sticks
- makeshift sticks
- wooden sticks
- metal sticks

## Word History of Arnis

For all intents and purposes, arnis, eskrima and kali all refer to the same family of Filipino weapon-based martial arts and fighting systems.

Both *Arnis* and *Eskrima* are loans from Spanish

**Arnis** comes from *arnés*, Old Spanish for *armor* (*harness* is an archaic English term for armor, which comes from the same roots as the Spanish term). It is said to derive from the armor costumes used in moro-moro stage plays where actors fought mock battles using wooden swords.*Arnes* is also an archaic Spanish term for weapon, like in the following sentence from *"Ilustracion de la Deztreza Indiana"* by Francisco Santos de la Paz in 1712:

*"Siendo tan infalible la execucion desta doctrina, que no solo consigue ésta superioridad en concurso de armas iguales, sino tambien hallandose el contrario con la aparente ventaja de venir armado de los dos **arneses**, Espada, y Daga; pues aun con ellos experimenta la dificultad de resistir á esta Espada sola..."*

"The execution of this doctrine is so infallible, that not only does it prove its superiority in contests with equal arms, but also when finding the opponent with the apparent advantage of showing up armed with two **weapons**, sword and dagger. For, even armed with those, experience shows the difficulty of resisting the single sword used in this way..."

REFERENCE:

https://en.wikipedia.org/wiki/Arnis

# The Arnis Law

Republic Act No. 9850 of the Congress of the Philippines, approved on December 11, 2009 declares Arnis as the national sport and martial art of the Philippines for promoting patriotism, nationalism and appreciation of the role of national heroes and symbols in the historical development of the country. Because of this law, Arnis becomes a pre-requisite for P.E. classes in most colleges in the Philippines.

The body of the law is as follows :

**Fourteenth Congress, Third Regular Session**

Begun and held in Metro Manila, on Monday, the twenty-seventh day of July, two thousand nine.

**Republic Act No. 9850**

**AN ACT DECLARING ARNIS AS THE NATIONAL MARTIAL ART AND SPORT OF THE PHILIPPINES**

*Be it enacted by the Senate and House of Representatives of the Philippines in Congress assembled:*

**Section 1.** It is the policy of the State to inculcate patriotism, nationalism and appreciation of the role of national heroes and symbols in the historical development of the country. Furthermore, the State must give priority to education, science and technology, arts and culture, and sports to foster patriotism and nationalism, accelerate social progress, and promote total human liberation and development.

**Section 2.** *Definition of Arnis.* - Arnis, also known as *Eskrima, Kali, Garrote* and other names in various regional languages, such as *Pananandata* in Tagalog; *Pagkalikali*, Ibanag; *Kabaraon* and *Kalirongan*, Pangasinan; *Kaliradman*, Bisaya; and *Didja*, Ilokano, is an indigenous Filipino martial art and sport characterized by the use of swinging and twirling movements, accompanied by striking, thrusting and parrying techniques for defense and offense. This is usually done with the use of one (1) or two (2) sticks or any similar implements or with bare hands and feet also used for striking, blocking, locking and grappling, with the use of the same principle as that with the canes.

**Section 3.** Arnis is hereby declared as the Philippine National Martial Art and Sport. The official adoption of arnis as the national martial art and sport shall be promulgated by inscribing the symbol of arnis in the official seal of the Philippine Sports Commission and by making it as the first sport competition to be played by participating teams on the first day in the annual Palarong Pambansa. The Philippine Sports Commission shall be the lead agency to implement the provisions of this Act.

**Section 4.** The Department of Education, the National Commission for Culture and the Arts, and the Philippine Sports Commission shall promulgate the necessary rules and regulations to carry out the provisions of this Act.

**Section 5.** Any provision of law, decree, executive order, rule or regulation in conflict or inconsistent with the provisions and/or purposes of this Act is hereby repealed, amended or modified accordingly.

**Section 6.** This Act shall take effect fifteen (15) days after its complete publication in the Official Gazette or in at least two (2) newspapers of general circulation.

Approved,

**Prospero C. Nograles, Speaker of the House of Representatives**

**Juan Ponce Enrile, President of the Senate**

This Act which is a consolidation of Senate Bill No. 3288 and House Bill No. 6516 was finally passed by the Senate and the House of Representatives on October 14, 2009.

**Marilyn B. Barua-Yap, Secretary General House of Representatives**

**Emma Lirio-Reyes, Secretary of the Senate**

Approved: December 11, 2009

**Gloria Macapagal-Arroyo, President of the Philippines**

REFERENCES:

http://www.lawphil.net/statutes/repacts/ra2009/ra_9850_2009.html

https://en.wikipedia.org/wiki/Arnis

http://sports.inquirer.net/sport/martialarts/view/20100122-248713/Govt-sports-officials-hail-Arnis-Law

http://www.arnisphilippines.com/

http://www.seasite.niu.edu/Tagalog/Modules/Modules/escrima/eskrima.htm

The Arnis Law

## About the Author

Angelo Tiwana Quiamco was born in Iloilo, Philippines. He was a Philippine author, critic, poet, anthropologist, essayist, and novelist. He graduated in Tigbauan Central Elementary School (2008) and passed in Alternative Learning System A&E Secondary Level (2013) where he got *SS 110 and ER 3.* He is a versatile writer; he is at home in writing poetry, fiction, and essay.

He is currently a freelance writer in different online publication; member of American Writers and Artist Inc. He was a practitioner of Arnis (Philippine National Martial Art and Sport) and TaeKwonDo, a Korean Martial Art and Sport.

For more information about him and his activities may contact to:

angelotiwana_quiamco@yahoo.com

eruditauruspolychrestysophilia@gmail.com

Notes

# Notes

Notes

# Notes